Adjectives Say "Incredible!"

by Michael Dahl   illustrated by Lauren Lowen

PICTURE WINDOW BOOKS
a capstone imprint

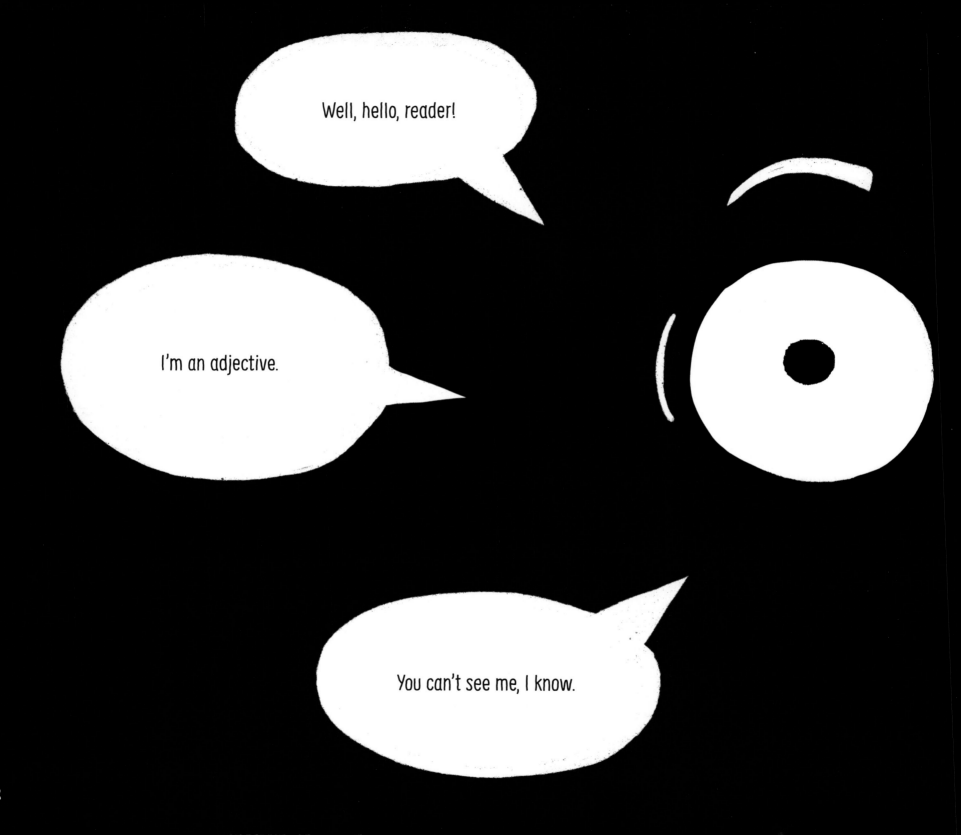

Adjectives describe nouns. Nouns are words that name people, places, and things.

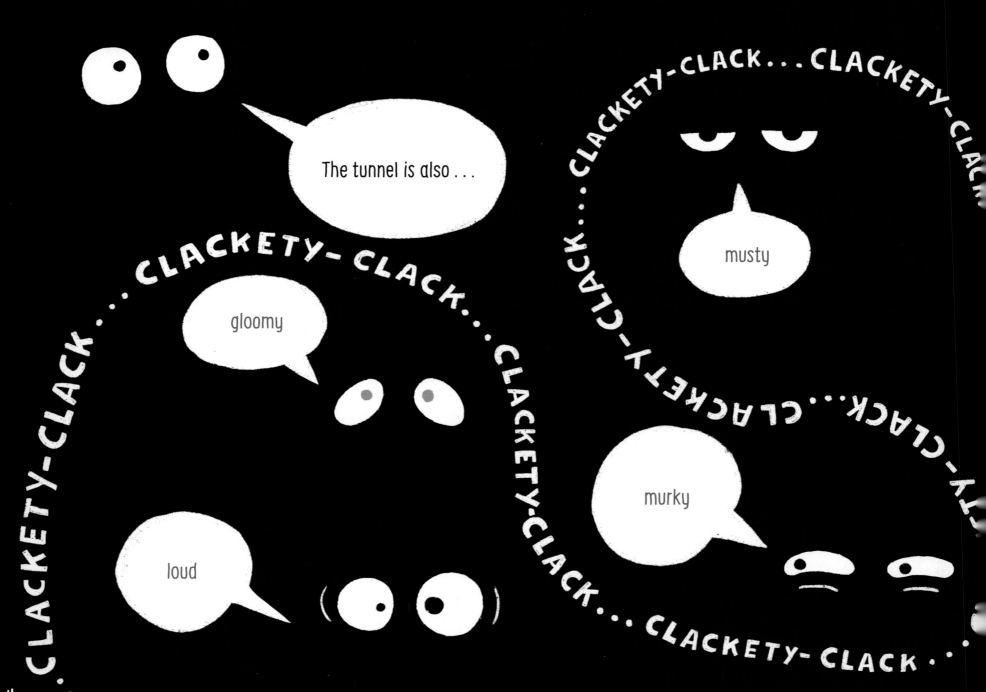

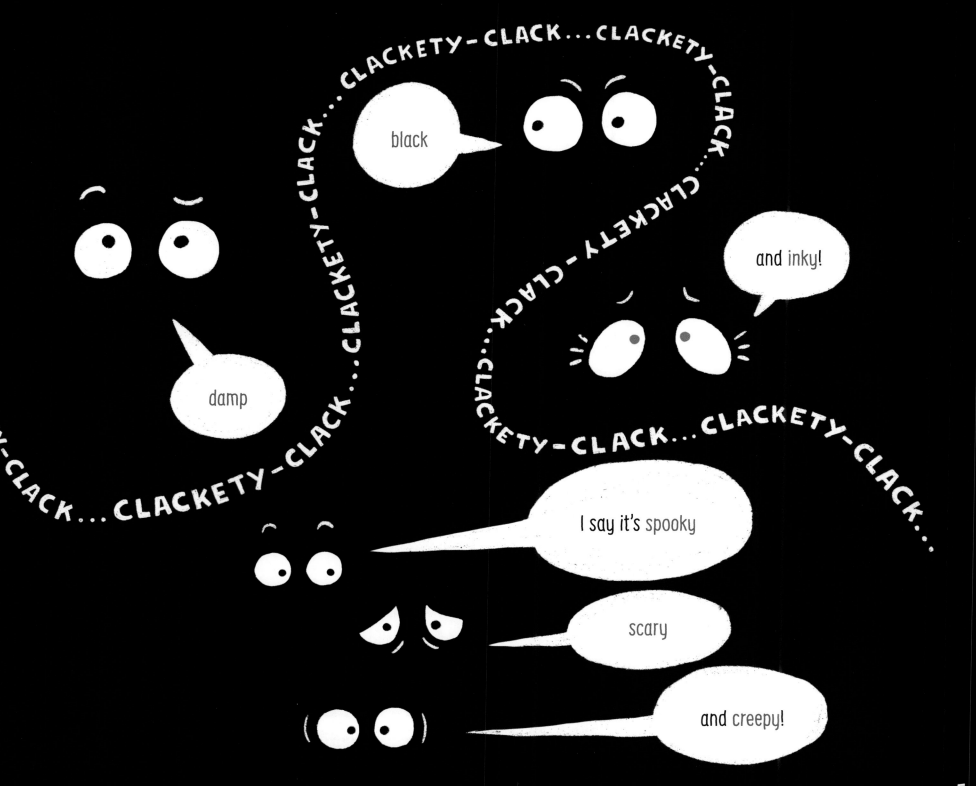

Adjectives describe how the world looks, smells, sounds, tastes, and feels.

I can see the giant sign! Just a few minutes to go!

Will there be furry, fuzzy, and feathered animals at the zoo?

Yep, squawking, growling, and roaring ones too.

SNIFF

9

In many sentences, adjectives are found in front of the nouns they describe.

15

Some adjectives mean the same thing.

You can spot some adjectives by the way they end.

23

You can use many adjectives to describe one thing.

This has been an awesome, tiring, surprising, incredible, happy, fabulous, amazing, tasty,

EXIT

COME BACK SOON!

ZOO

UGH

24

Or you can use one single, perfect adjective.

It was wonderful!

ALL ABOUT AWESOME ADJECTIVES

Adjectives are words that describe nouns. Nouns are people, places, and things.

a friendly bus driver ("friendly" describes a person)
a noisy, crowded lunchroom ("noisy" and "crowded" describe a place)
a brilliant and twinkling star ("brilliant" and "twinkling" describe a thing)

Adjectives tell us how something looks, sounds, smells, feels, or tastes.

a purple racecar
a rumbling storm
some stinky socks
the wet icicle
my sweet, delicious ice-cream cone

Some adjectives are numbers. They tell us how many nouns there are.

one gorilla
five puppies

Adjectives can compare nouns to one another.

The bear is tall.
The tree is taller.
The mountain is tallest.

ABOUT THE AUTHOR

Michael Dahl is the author of more than 200 books for children and has won the AEP Distinguished Achievement Award three times for his nonfiction. He is the author of the bestselling *Bedtime for Batman* and *You're a Star, Wonder Woman!* picture books. He has written dozens of books of jokes, riddles, and puns. He likes to play with words. In grade school, he read the dictionary for fun. Really. Michael is proud to say that he has always been a noun. A PROPER noun, at that.

ABOUT THE ILLUSTRATOR

Since graduating from the Illustration Department at the Rhode Island School of Design (RISD), **Lauren Lowen** has been creating art for a variety of projects, including publishing, ad campaigns, and products ranging from greeting cards and stickers to activity books and kids' luggage. She taught illustration at both Montserrat College of Art and RISD before becoming an instructor at Watkins College of Art in Nashville, Tennessee, where she currently lives with her husband and son. Some of her favorite things include sushi, chocolate milk, and Star Trek.

GLOSSARY

adjective—a word that tells more about a noun or pronoun

compare—to look closely at things to discover ways they are alike or different

describe—to tell about something

noun—a word that names a person, place, or thing

THINK ABOUT IT

1. The word "hot" is an adjective. What other words do you know that have the same meaning as "hot"?

2. What adjectives could you use to describe your favorite animal? Think about how it looks, sounds, and smells.

3. How would you finish the following sentence? **My best friend is _____.** Use at least six adjectives.

READ MORE

Ayers, Linda. *Bumpy, Bright, Blue: What Adjectives Do!* Read, Sing, Learn: Songs About the Parts of Speech. Minneapolis: Cantata Learning, 2016.

Heinrichs, Ann, and Danielle Jacklin. *Adjectives.* Language Rules. New York: AV2 by Weigl, 2018.

Loewen, Nancy. *The Big Problem (and the Squirrel Who Eventually Solved It): Understanding Adjectives and Adverbs.* Language on the Loose. North Mankato, MN: Picture Window Books, a Capstone imprint, 2016.

INTERNET SITES

Enchanted Learning: Grammar: Adjectives
https://www.enchantedlearning.com/grammar/partsofspeech/adjectives/index.shtml

Grammaropolis: The Adjectives
https://www.grammaropolis.com/adjective.php

Schoolhouse Rock: Adjectives
https://www.youtube.com/watch?v=NkuuZEey_bs

LOOK FOR ALL THE PARTS OF SPEECH TITLES

INDEX

Editor: Jill Kalz
Designer: Lori Bye
Production Specialist: Katy LaVigne
The illustrations in this book were created digitally.

Picture Window Books are published by Capstone
1710 Roe Crest Drive, North Mankato, Minnesota 56003
www.capstonepub.com

Library of Congress Cataloging-in-Publication Data is available on the Library of Congress website.
ISBN 978-1-5158-3871-5 (library binding)
ISBN 978-1-5158-4060-2 (paperback)
ISBN 978-1-5158-3876-0 (eBook PDF)
Summary: It's Zoo Day, and the adjectives can't wait for all the furry, fuzzy, feathered, noisy, wet, and sweet things. The perfect pairing of solid grammar basics and plenty of goofiness, this illustrated parts-of-speech adventure teaches and entertains all at once. Incredible!

All internet sites appearing in back matter were available and accurate when this book was sent to press.

Printed and bound in the United States of America.
112019   002943